Communities in Time

Airedale & Ferry Fryston · Eastmoor · Knottingley & Ferrybridge · Portobello

Fryston Colliery Workers

Communities in Time
Participating groups and organisations by area:

Airedale and Ferry Fryston
Airedale Friends
Airedale Junior School
Airedale Library & visitors
Holy Cross Companionship Group
Oyster Park Junior School
South West Yorkshire Partnership NHS Foundation Trust
Wakefield District Housing

Eastmoor
Eastmoor Community Archive
ERA (Eastmoor Resident Arts)
Next Generation
Simply Leisure

Knottingley and Ferrybridge
Knottingley Library & visitors
Old Quarry Adventure Playground
South West Yorkshire Partnership NHS Foundation Trust
St Botolph's Church
Wakefield District Housing

Portobello
Portobello Community Forum
Rainbow Café visitors
Soul Portobello

Communities in Time
First published in United Kingdom 2013 by Faceless Company
Unit E Fox Way, Trinity Business Park Wakefield WF2 8EE.

www.facelessco.com

Text © Faceless Company 2013
Book Design and Illustrations © John Welding 2013
Photographs © The individual owners

ISBN: 978-0-9568436-2-3

Communities in Time

Airedale & Ferry Fryston · Eastmoor · Knottingley & Ferrybridge · Portobello

Faceless
*exceptional arts experiences
for everyone ... everywhere*

Communities in Time Introduction

In 2012 The Faceless Company delivered a series of creative community projects which explored peoples' personal experiences of community history. The company looked at how people, places and events shaped different areas of Wakefield and explored common themes and linkages.

Communities in Time was a trans-generational project looking at community cohesion and pride of place and was funded by Wakefield Council through their Creative Partners programme.

Artists from Faceless travelled to Eastmoor, Portobello, Knottingley & Ferrybridge and Airedale & Ferry Fryston to deliver workshops for the project. Working with around 300 people from across all four areas, participants were aged 5 - 96 and came to the project from a variety of backgrounds.

Before we began, we researched each of the four areas and created timelines of significant historical events that we could take into communities to spark conversations about how these events related to individuals and their families within each area.

We wanted to create something people could be proud of - a visual record of people's thoughts and memories which could be treasured by them and also displayed for both their communities and the wider public to see and enjoy.

To this end, we collected information from a wide range of community members and added this to the historical timelines to give context... to events within each community. Some of this information can be found in this book, along with personal and public photographs and art work created by project participants.

We used silk painting workshops, to visualise our timelines in a way that was relevant to individuals, and showed the importance of particular events, buildings, people and places to those communities. These images, created by community members from inspirational source material gathered in the community, were then collated into wall hangings by artists at Faceless; and can be seen hanging in community buildings, within the communities that made them. We used tree imagery for the project, as we felt the roots, trunk and growing, changing foliage provided a good metaphor for how the communities have grown and changed over the years.

The response to the project was very positive, with many events and personal remembrances added to the community timelines and over 150 community paintings being created during the sessions in each area.

This book stands, not as an historical record, but as a record of our project. It is designed to give a flavour of each community; of their identity within the District; and to share with you some of the stories and remembrances that the members of these 4 unique communities have chosen to share with us on our journey into the past.

Faceless

exceptional arts experiences
for everyone ... everywhere

Airedale & Ferry Fryston

Wendy Johnson remembers a trip to Fryston Pit during the 1960s...

"After falling and cutting open my hand, instead of a visit to the hospital to have it stitched, I was taken to Fryston pit to see Sister Thorpe, the Colliery Nurse, who stitched it there and then."

"I used to go to the pit with my Grandad on Friday when he got his wages and he gave me a thrupenny bit."

Olivia Scales, who was born in 2000 and has lived in Airedale all her life, told us her Grandad worked in the pit. Harry Jones' Grandad also worked in the pit, as did Isabella Parker's.

In the **1930s** Henry Moore's father was an under-manager at Weldale Colliery. Moore himself sketched the workers there during the second world war.

Reproduced by permission of The Henry Moore Foundation

Dot, Chris and Marie remember...

"There were more than 6 pits in the Airedale area, with 28 across the wider area. By the end of the Miners' Strikes in the 1980s there were just 3. Job losses changed the area massively, there was no natural employer for young people coming out of schools."

Jim Westgarth, an Airedale resident left the army in 1984. He remembers looking for work in Airedale when he left school...

"I was born in Airedale and my Grandad wouldn't let me work down the pit, he said it was too dangerous, so I went into the army. Dad worked for Remploy and Lewis' Ice Cream van based in Knottingley."

Jack Shepherd's Dad and Grandparents have lived in Airedale all their lives. His Grandad's Dad worked at the pit and died because of all the coal he inhaled.

Junior school pupil Alex Wardle's Grandad moved here to work in the pits in the 1960s. His Great Great Grandad fought in World War One. He knows that Glasshoughton pit became Xscape in 2003, and now employs a lot of local people.

"I was born at St Peter's and went to Fryston School."

"I liked going to St Peter's because the organ was loud and you could have a right good sing song."

"I remember the last service at St Peter's."

St Peter's Church was built in Fryston by the community in 1896 and was demolished in 1991 when the pit closed.

In 1086, Fryston was named in the Doomsday Book.

In 1934, Holy Cross Church was built and remains an important part of the community today.

1870 Weldale Colliery was founded and in 1873 Fryston Colliery was sunk. Fryston closed 1985, Glasshoughton closed 1986.

In 2007, a former pupil of Airedale High School was killed in Afghanistan aged 18. The funeral was held at Holy Cross Church and hundreds of mourners and ex-servicemen attended.

In August 2011, a memorial wall was unveiled at Airedale Academy.

Silk Painting workshop participant working on an image of the Fryston War Memorial

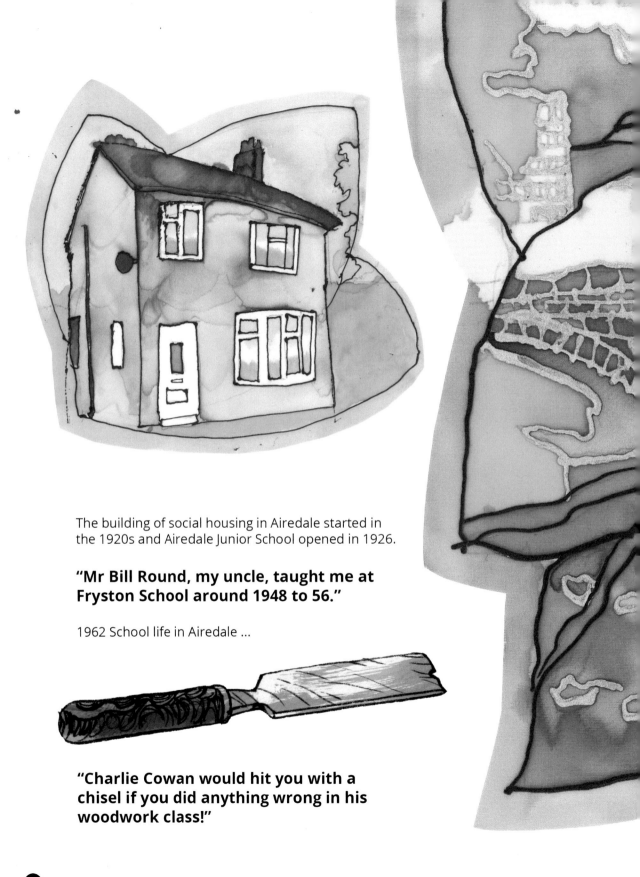

The building of social housing in Airedale started in the 1920s and Airedale Junior School opened in 1926.

"Mr Bill Round, my uncle, taught me at Fryston School around 1948 to 56."

1962 School life in Airedale ...

"Charlie Cowan would hit you with a chisel if you did anything wrong in his woodwork class!"

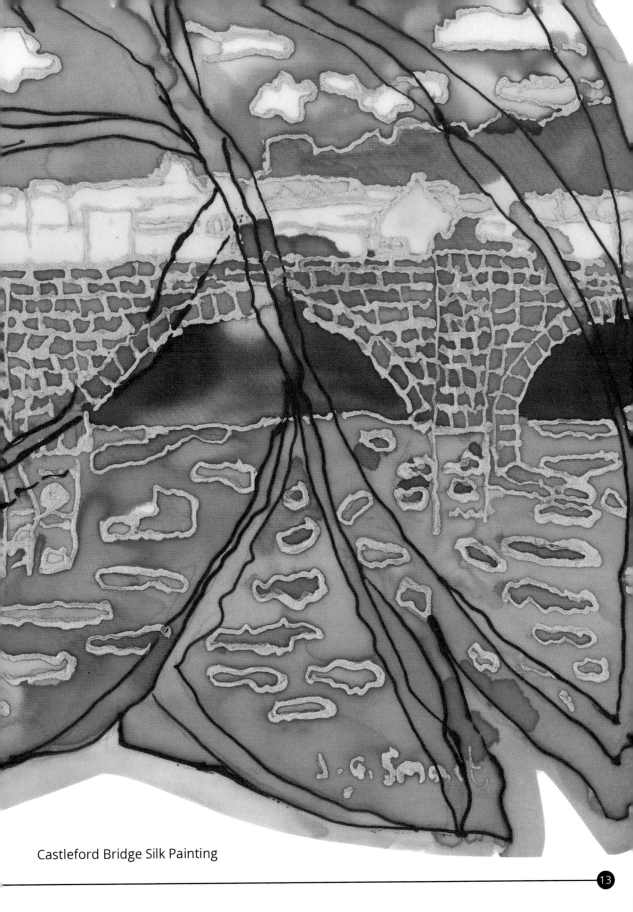

Castleford Bridge Silk Painting

Ron Faulkes remembers life on the estate in the fifties.

"Gilligan would come with a horse and cart which had a wind up roundabout on the back and you would give a rag or a jam jar or penny and he would turn it around."

Jack Hulme photographed Gilligan earning his living.

© Wakefield Council

"In 1995, my Dad's school burnt down and he had to work in a horrid wooden hut."

In June 2003, Airedale High School was attacked by arsonists for a second time.

In 2003, the Airedale Centre & Library opened.

In 2005, the High School was attacked for the third time, and after this, a state of the art theatre was built and opened in 2008 (Castleford Phoenix Theatre).

on 1 April 2011, the school converted to academy status.

Eastmoor

In 1995, the Eastmoor Community Project was founded on the Eastmoor Housing Estate. The project went on to build the St Swithun's Community Centre, which officially opened in 2003. It is a hub for the local community and hosts groups such as Simply Leisure, a weekly group for over 55s.

"My husband and I down-sized and came to live on Eastmoor in 2009. I love it and have met so many friends by joining Simply Leisure at the St Swithun's Centre. We have lots of laughs."

Maureen – **"The estate went up to house hospital workers, railway engineering workers and mining families. Houses were allocated to workers from certain workplaces. When people were moved into the estate from slum clearances, they brought established communities and extended families into the area."**

1990s
The Queen visits Wakefield to open a new nursery building at St Mary's School.

Local resident Molly Farrar remembers being given the task of getting flowers for her visit.

With flowers from Warrengate Flower shop, Molly created a table decoration, as well as a posy to be given to the Queen by a child.

1877 Parkhill Colliery opened... it closed in 1983.

Ann Dexter remembers...

"I can remember when my children were small and Parkhill Colliery was still a working pit. We walked from Parkhill Crescent down Park Lodge Lane and down the mud track to the strawberry fields, picked strawberries and walked back. The strawberry fields are now a part of Pinders Heath Estate."

1740 Aire and Calder navigation opened between Leeds and Knottingley.

Brian – **"Canal boats were still moving coal on Tom Puddings around Eastmoor until the 1960s."**

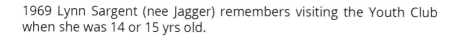

1969 Lynn Sargent (nee Jagger) remembers visiting the Youth Club when she was 14 or 15 yrs old.

"I went with my friend Susan. She met her childhood sweetheart there, his name was Sam. They went out together a long time. One evening we had someone in talking to us about venereal diseases. It really opened our eyes, some of the slides they showed us!"

1846 St Andrew's Church, Peterson Road is built.

In the 1970s, Mary Milsom's son was married here. Anne was christened here in the 40s, as were her children in the 60s and 70s.

Maureen – **"Lots of women from Eastmoor Estate worked at Stanley Royd as the hours were flexible and they could work around their husband's and family's needs."**

Stanley Royd Asylum for Pauper Lunatics opened to patients in 1818. It finally closed in 1996 and is now a housing estate.

Building began in 1867 on the Pinderfields Hospital site. It was originally part of the West Riding Pauper Lunatic Asylum. It was built to house recently diagnosed mental patients, keeping them totally separate in an entirely new building. In 2011, the old hospital closed and the name has now passed to the new hospital which stands next to the old site.

In 1948, the maternity unit closed as it was transferred to Manygates Hospital. The ward became an elderly care facility. On its closure, nurses were deployed to Clayton, Pinderfields and Fieldhead Hospitals.

Marie was a nurse at Pinderfields from 1962 until she retired. In 1995 she shook Princess Diana's hand when she visited the Second Chance Unit.

Knottingley & Ferrybridge

1794 Knottingley Pottery was established. It became Ferrybridge Pottery in 1804. In 1938, a young girl aged 14 began her working life at the firm.

"I started age 14 in 1938, earned 10 shillings a week. Lots of people worked there. There's a lot goes in to making a pot, from the raw clay to the finished product. I started as a mould runner, hanging out the clay for the maker to make pots, then I went on to be a maker. I worked in biscuit ware and glass ware. We made plant pots with a brown glaze, food bowls with a blue stripe – the stripe was blown on by hand with a tube. I had to carry bowls on a 6 foot board – the number underneath the bowl meant how many of that size would fit on the board. I enjoyed going to work. I was 61 when I finished. I met my husband there. It wasn't love at first sight. When he went into the army and wrote to his sister he put a letter in for me. I was really surprised. We were married 42 years. During the war, every window had to be blacked out. We moved on to gas and electric ovens after the War. Nothing was wasted, materials were reused or recycled.

Jackson's Glassworks was established in 1893 by two former Bagley's apprentices Tom and John Jackson. **"I started in 1938. I worked at Jackson's in the warehouse, George Baxter taught me to sort the boxes onto the leer* pack up the good ones, sort out the crizzles*. There were complaints if a customer got a 'birdcage'*. There was no heating in winter so I wore my coat and scarf. We earned 10 shillings a week."**

In 1962, Jackson's took over the Bagley Glass Factory
"I worked at Jacksons in the 1970s, Bagley's didn't employ women – it was all men and two of us women were taken to Bagley's, to the shrink wrap department, by an escort who stayed with us all night. After that they employed women in the glass painting section."

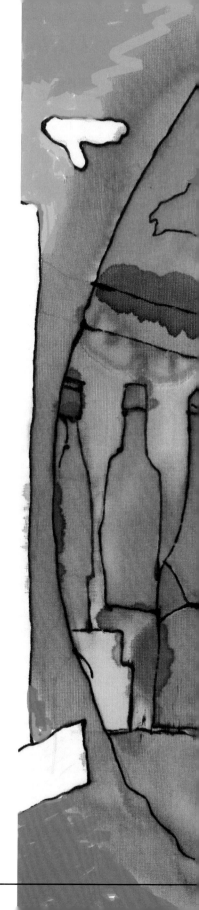

*birdcage: A reject bottle with a ridge of glass on the inside
*crizzle: A mis-shapen bottle   *leer: Conveyor belt

1965
Ferrybridge power station was first built in 1926 and the station began operating in 1927.The original station (A) closed on 25 October 1976, the boiler room and turbine hall are still standing and are currently used as offices and workshops. The second incarnation (Ferrybridge B) was constructed in the 1950s, this closed in 1992 and has been completely demolished.

Ferrybridge C made of eight towers, was built in the 1960s, on 1 November 1965, three of the cooling towers collapsed in high winds. The shape that the cooling towers were built in meant that the wind was pulled between the towers, creating a vortex. Three out of the original eight cooling towers were destroyed and the remaining five were severely damaged. The towers were rebuilt and all eight towers were strengthened to better tolerate adverse weather conditions.

1950 "...The Wagon and Horses, The Book, The Threepenny Scratch, there used to be loads of pubs in Knottingley. You could go on a pub crawl down Aire Street. Tucker's Fair used to be down there, there was the Rat Trap, that's now an old folk's home ; there was the Jolly – that's still there; there was the L+Y next to the railway. We used to go in there when the landlord was in bed; we used to pull our own pint and leave the money on the bar. There was the Commercial, my friend used to come round to mine at night with her rollers in. She told her husband we were having a quiet night in, the men were on nights, as soon as they went to work, we used to take our rollers out put our make-up on and go down the pub. I went out one night and we were sitting in the cemetery. When I got home I'd got somebody's date of birth printed on my bottom!"

In 1958, my husband used to go to the cinema (the chapel on Aire Street) to watch the westerns – all the kids would come out slapping their bottoms and yelping!

In 1962, Carol Buckley remembers...

"Once a week you would have groceries delivered from Claude Spence's shop, you would write your order in a book. A man used to come round and sharpen knives every so often, and on a Sunday a man used to come round pushing a barrow selling Wall's ice cream."

Knottingley silk painting workshop participants

1843 Gunfighter Ben Thompson was born in Knottingley. He was gunned down in a saloon bar in America in 1884.

1850 A through route to London by railway via Knottingley is opened in 1850. In 1879, the Swinton & Knottingley railway is opened.

Susan Atfield's Grandfather Albert Rush (pictured), was Knottingley Station Master c. 1890 – 1910.

An ex-teacher from Knottingley remembers working on the Warwick Estate before the school was built. Her school originally had 3 empty classrooms but as people moved down from Scotland and the North East for mining jobs. These rooms filled up and eventually, even the staff room had to be used for teaching children.

1972 The Old Quarry Adventure opened on Warwick Estate. The only adventure playground in Wakefield district, it continues to develop as a playground and community resource.

2003 Throstle Farm School closed, it was built on the Warwick Estate in the 1960s to accommodate the growing population of families with children.

1960s A Knottingley resident remembers...

"I remember the submarine coming up the canal I think it was the Dreadnaught, it was a miniature submarine and it came up the canal to get the 'Freedom of the City' in Leeds. You couldn't see submarine, only the man stood on top!

Portobello

1157 Sandal Castle fortifications began in stone, it was destroyed along with that of Pontefract in 1648.

1460 Yorkist, Richard Plantagenet, marched his men to Sandal Castle before he was killed at the battle of Wakefield giving origin to Nursery Rhyme "The Grand Old Duke of York".

1921 Portobello, Wakefield's first major housing estate was built with street names from events in the Boer War, such as Pretoria & Kimberley Street.

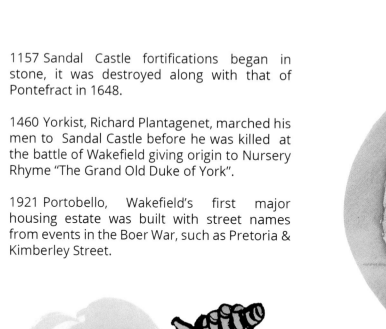

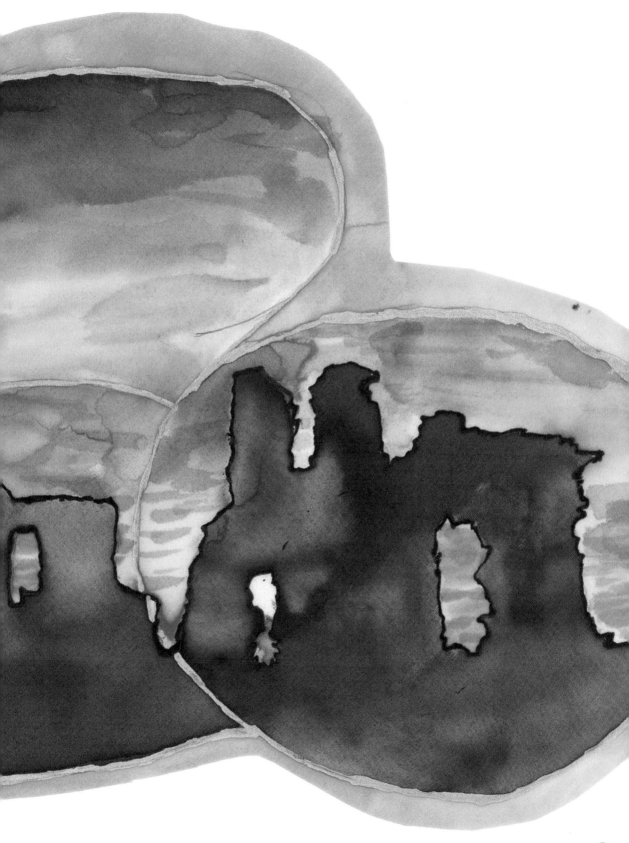

1986 The Victory club formed, providing activities for elderly people at the Youth and Community Centre.

2010 The La Twirl Tastique Majorette Troupe formed and received a grant for £1000 from Wakefield District Housing to support their work with young people.

2012 A stone mural depicting the nursery rhyme "The Grand Old Duke of York" was designed and created by young people from Portobello alongside artist Dan Jones, in a project by Groundwork Wakefield.

In 2012, Leaf Sculptures were laid at Portobello shops.

1849
Manygates House was built. In 1934, it was bought as the site of the Manygates Maternity Hospital. It was then extended and adapted for staff accommodation. It later became a Halls of Residence and is currently part of the Woodlands Village development which was realised in 2007.

"The women liked Manygates Hospital because you could walk up. Was very upset when that got closed."

"I was born in Manygates Maternity Hospital on 11th February 1946."

Claire remembers...

"I lived at Manygates during my first year at uni. It was the first year that it was a student hall of residence."

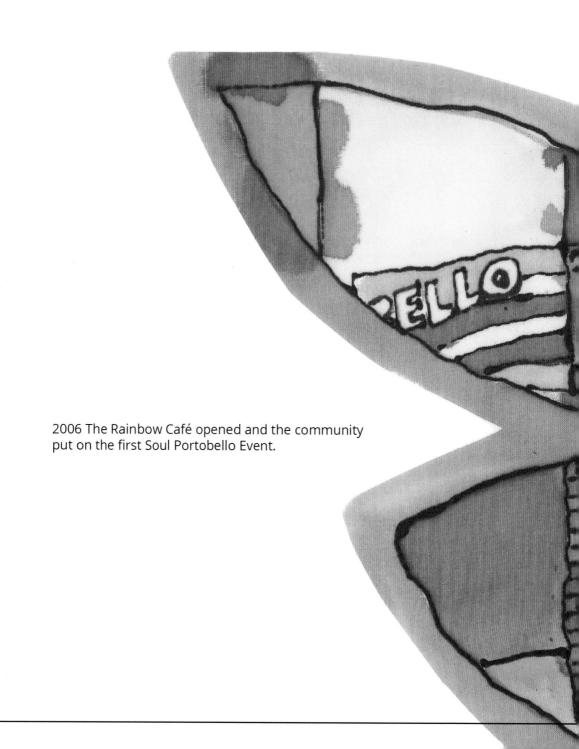

2006 The Rainbow Café opened and the community put on the first Soul Portobello Event.

1928 Manygates School opened. In 1978, Javed Iqbal moved to Wakefield from Pakistan and went to Manygates School.

"I started in the third year or fourth year of Manygates Middle School. First day I went to school, I can still remember it was snowing and all the English lads and the Pakistani lads were just snowball fighting and sliding and playing games and sliding all over. I was just frozen to one spot 'cause I were that cold. I can still remember (being) stood at the side of the science block crying me eyes out.

One of the teachers came over and said "What's wrong with you" and I couldn't tell her that I was cold 'cause I couldn't speak English, so she got a Pakistani girl to come over and ask me "What's wrong with you?" and I said "I'm just cold". So she explained that I was new, and the teacher, bless her, took me inside, put me hands under warm water and for the next three months I was told if it's too cold I can stay inside. So I went into the corridor and found a best friend called the radiator and for the next three months when it was snowing or raining or whatever, I stayed inside near the radiator."

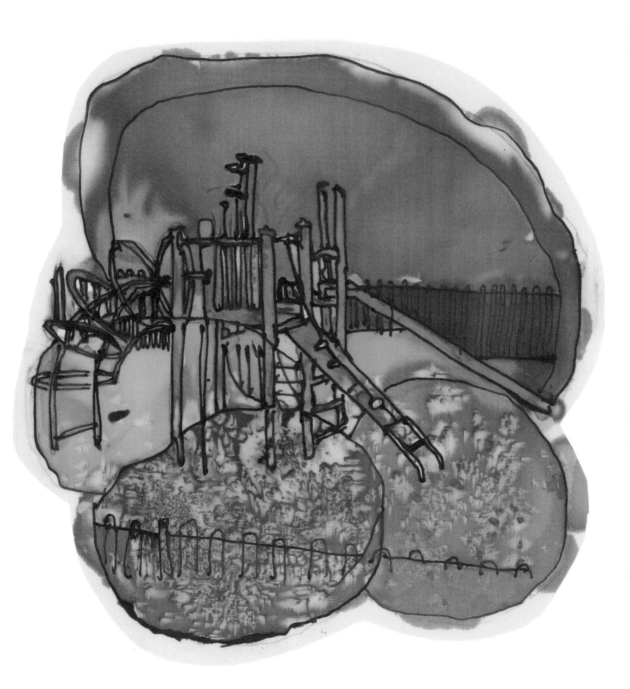

Portobello playground Silk Painting

Timelines for the communities of Airedale & Ferry Fryston,
Eastmoor, Knottingley & Ferrybridge and Portobello
interpreted as four different tree wall hangings.

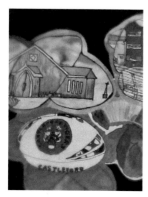

Communities
in Time

Airedale & Ferry Fryston · Eastmoor · Knottingley & Ferrybridge · Portobello

Faceless
exceptional arts experiences
for everyone ... everywhere

wakefield council
working for you